This book is dedicated to :
My mother, my godmother, and grandmother, who gave me the gifts of faith and creativity as a child. May these be the same gifts I give to my son.
Melinda Murphy, who is not only an amazing friend but a beautiful writer –Melinda graciously wrote and donated the "Opening Activity", "Jesus Connection", and "Prayer" sections of this book. You are a wonderful person, and I am so thankful to have the opportunity to do this project with you!
My husband, Andy. Thank you for always believing in me, being there for me, and never complaining about the craft supplies that are slowly overtaking the house. You are my man, and I love you.

FAITH
and
Fabric

TABLE of Contents

FAITH and Fabric

BEFORE you Start

- **FOR KINDLE USERS ONLY**: The templates in this book can be downloaded and printed from the site below
  - **SITE**: http://wp.me/P6tEFb-Wr
  - **PASSWORD**: jessetreekindle

- Please read all instructions carefully before starting to cut, glue, or sew.

- The instructions in the book are for making the ornaments out of felt and sewing them together. However, the ornaments can actually be made many different ways depending on how much time you have, who is making the ornaments, etc. See "Gather Your Materials" to determine the method that is best for you. **TIP**: if you're cutting the templates from felt, paper, or craft foam, save your small scrap pieces as you'll be able to use them for other ornaments.

Color or Paint the Coloring Sheets	Cut from Craft Foam or Construction Paper	Cut from Felt and Glue or Hand Stitch

- Each of the ornament templates in this book are meant to be a guide; as they are hand drawn, variations in line thickness, edges, and lengths will naturally occur. I was inspired to draw these by hand and not by computer to preserve some of the natural flows, movements, stutters, and beautiful imperfections that come with hand drawn (vs. perfectly digitized) designs. I stayed away from rulers for straight edges and templates for perfect circles as part of this philosophy. It just seems...more of true "artwork" that way. You are welcome to use the designs exactly "as is" or to adjust based on what works for you.

FAITH and Fabric

BEFORE you Start

- Where possible, the names of the pieces and corresponding colors will print directly on the piece that needs to be cut. This will help identify the pieces once you cut them out, as well as what color paper/foam/felt needs to be cut from that template.

- This is a project of art. You are encouraged to adapt and create something beautiful, with these templates serving only as a guide – and never a limit - to your creativity.

- This is also – and most importantly - a project of faith. A short scripture verse is included with each ornament, giving context to what that specific ornament represents. If using this as an eBook, you can click on the scripture reading, which will take you to a fuller text for that specific verse. Families are encouraged to use their own family or children's story Bible for the readings as subtle variations do occur within Biblical translations and within denominations. *Note:* This book was a collaborative effort between two Christians of different denominations. Every effort has been made to correctly represent Biblical teachings, but please – as the parent and teachers of your children – rephrase or modify the activities, readings, Jesus connections, and prayers as appropriate to your family.

- As this is a Jesse Tree, and tells the story from Old to New Testament of Jesus and his fulfillment of prophecy, each day has a section tying in how that day's theme connects to Jesus. You will see Jesus as a prominent theme throughout this book.

- Don't stress if you miss a devotion or an activity on a certain day.

- If your children are too young to think of a prayer on their own, have them repeat your prayer each phrase at a time. This is a great way of helping them learn how to pray.

BEFORE you Start

- The days of the book are broken into three parts:

Daily Activities & Devotions

Instructions & Photos

Coloring Sheets & Cut-Out Templates

DAY 1: Creation/Earth

Opening Activity: Take a walk or go out in the backyard and point out different things that God created. Look closely at different colors, leaves, grass, trees and flowers. Talk about how detailed and creatively God made the world.

Reading: God saw all that he had made, and it was very good. Thus the heavens and the earth were completed in all their vast array. (Genesis 1:31, 2)

Symbol: Earth

Summary: God, who always was and always will be, created the whole world in six days, resting on the seventh day. Everything he made is good and has value, including man and woman which he made in his image.

Jesus Connection: In Genesis 1:26, God says, "Let us make man in OUR image." God the Father, God the Son, and God the Holy Spirit were all involved in making our world! In fact, when Paul is talking about Jesus in Colossians 1:16, he says that "all things have been created through Him and for Him." So before God the Son came down to earth to be Jesus, He made the world!

Prayer: What are some of your favorite things that God made? I want us to each take a turn to pray and thank God for something He created.

DAY 1: Creation/Earth

Materials:
- embroidery needles
- stuffing
- scissors
- felt in blue & green
- embroidery floss blue & green
- background music: He's Got the Whooooole World in His Hands

How to Make:
- OCEANS: cut out two circles from the blue felt (one for the back and one for the front of the ornament).
- CONTINENTS: cut out the continents from the green felt. Arrange the continents on one of the blue ocean circles, taking the edges of the continents right up to the edges of your circle. Using green floss, stitch the continents – as close to the edge of the continent as you can – onto the blue circle (ocean).
- ATTACHING FRONT TO BACK: blanket stitch the two oceans together using a blanket stitch. Make a tiny blanket stitch behind the continents and keep it longer/more visible on the ocean. Be sure to add some stuffing just before you sew it closed!

DAY 1: Creation/Earth

CONTINENTS (green)

OCEANS (blue)

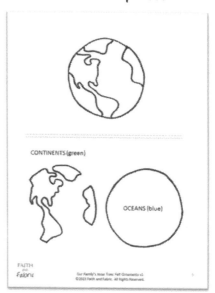

GATHER your Materials

There are many ways to make these ornaments; listed below are five possibilities (though there are probably even more!).

1. **Color Your Own Ornaments**: if coloring is perfect for you, the ornaments can be printed out on a thicker paper / cardstock and colored with crayons, markers, colored pencils, or any other medium. This is a great option for kids of all ages! If coloring, materials include:
   - scissors
   - crayons
   - cardstock (recommended for printing ornaments so they will be sturdy)
   - ribbon (for attaching ornament to tree)
   - glue gun (for attaching ribbon to ornament)

2. **Make Paper Ornaments from Templates**: for those looking to work on cutting skills, the templates can be cut out and traced onto colored construction paper. Once cut out, the pieces can be assembled and glued together to make a custom ornament! If cutting and making paper ornaments, materials include:
   - scissors
   - construction paper
   - paper glue
   - ribbon (for attaching ornament to tree)
   - glue gun (for attaching ribbon to ornament)

3. **Make Foam Ornaments from Craft Foam**: for a more durable (and longer lasting) ornament, cutting from craft foam instead of construction paper is a great alternative. If cutting and making craft foam ornaments, materials include:
   - scissors
   - craft foam
   - craft foam glue
   - ribbon (for attaching ornament to tree)
   - glue gun (for attaching ribbon to ornament)

4. **Make Felt Ornaments with Fabric Glue**: felt is a beautiful option for creating your ornaments, and makes ornaments that will last for years to come. You can secure the felt together with fabric glue if sewing isn't your style. If cutting and gluing felt ornaments, materials include:
   - scissors
   - felt in assorted colors (I recommend getting a variety pack)
   - fabric glue
   - batting/stuffing
   - ribbon (for attaching ornament to tree)

5. **Make Felt Ornaments with Embroidery Floss**: creating the ornaments from felt and hand stitching them together makes gorgeous ornaments that become instant family heirlooms. If cutting and sewing felt ornaments, materials include:
   - scissors
   - felt in assorted colors (I recommend getting a variety pack)
   - embroidery floss in assorted colors (I recommend DMC variety pack)
   - embroidery needles (you'll need ones with the large eye in the needle)
   - batting/stuffing
   - ribbon (for attaching ornament to tree)

FAITH and Fabric

DAY 1: Creation/Earth

Opening Activity: Before the devotion, have your children gather some leaves, flowers, dirt, or other things that God created. Together, look closely at different colors and designs. Say: In our Bible story today, we're going to learn about God making our world.

Reading: God saw all that he had made, and it was very good. Thus the heavens and the earth were completed in all their vast array. (Genesis 1:1-2:3 or the story of creation)

Symbol: Earth

Summary: God, who always was and always will be, created the whole world in six days, resting on the seventh day. Everything He made is good and has value, including man and woman which he made in His image.

Jesus Connection: In Genesis 1:26, God says, "Let **US** make man in **OUR** image." God the Father, God the Son, and God the Holy Spirit were all involved in making our world! In fact, when Paul is talking about Jesus in Colossians 1:16, he says that "all things have been created through Him and for Him." So, before God the Son came down to earth to be Jesus, He made the world!

Prayer: What are some of your favorite things that God made? I want us to each take a turn to pray and thank God for something He created. (Example: Thank You, God, for making giraffes. Their long necks are really neat. I love You. Amen.)

DAY 1: Creation/Earth

Materials:

- embroidery needles
- stuffing
- scissors
- felt in blue & green
- embroidery floss blue & green
- background music: He's Got the Whole World in His Hands

How to Make:

- OCEANS: cut out two circles from the blue felt (one for the back and one for the front of the ornament).
- CONTINENTS: cut out the continents from the green felt. Arrange the continents on one of the blue ocean circles, taking the edges of the continents right up to the edges of your circle. Using green floss, stitch the continents – as close to the edge of the continent as you can – onto the blue circle (ocean).
- ATTACHING FRONT TO BACK: blanket stitch the two oceans together using a blanket stitch. Make a tiny blanket stitch behind the continents and keep it longer/more visible on the ocean. Be sure to add some stuffing just before you sew it closed!

CONTINENTS (green)

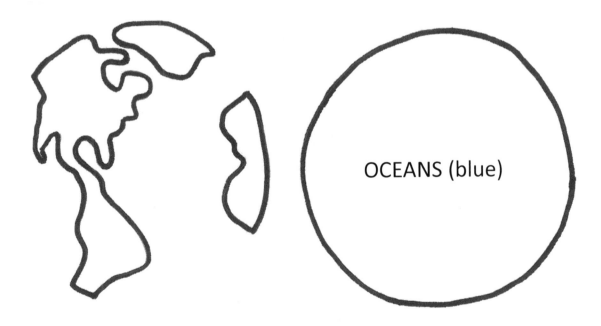

OCEANS (blue)

DAY 2: Adam & Eve / Apple

Opening Activity: Before the devotion, put a few different kinds of fruit in individual bags. Have the kids take turns reaching in the bag and guessing what kind of fruit is in each bag. Say: In our Bible story today, God tells Adam and Eve they can eat the fruit from any tree except from one. Let's find out what happens.

Reading: And the LORD God commanded the man, "You are free to eat from any tree in the garden; but you must not eat from the tree of the knowledge of good and evil, for when you eat from it you will certainly die." (Genesis 2-3:24 or the story of Adam and Eve)

Symbol: Apple

Summary: Adam and Eve were given a beautiful life in the Garden of Eden, and were made responsible for its care in accordance with God's instruction. His instruction included not eating from a tree in the center of the garden; they disobeyed God and were cast out of the garden.

Jesus Connection: Adam and Eve disobeyed God when Satan, disguised as a serpent, tricked them into eating the fruit off the tree God told them not to eat. Because they disobeyed, God punished them. He told them that it would be hard work to plant food; it would be difficult for Adam and Eve to get along; it would hurt to have babies; they would get old and die. We still have these problems today. But God also gave Adam and Eve a promise that brought hope. When talking to the serpent, God tells him that one day one of the children that comes from Eve will crush the serpent's head. This was the very first promise of Jesus in the Bible! Jesus will one day defeat Satan, just like God said.

After God punished Adam and Eve, He made clothes for them out of animal skins. Whenever God has animals sacrificed in the Bible, it is a secret message pointing to Jesus! The secret message is that one day Jesus, God the Son, would come to be the final sacrifice. He would die on the cross, taking the punishment for our sins, so that whoever believes in Him, will have eternal life. That means, they will have a right relationship with God both here on earth and forever with God in heaven.

DAY 2: Adam & Eve / Apple

Prayer: Sin is anything we think, say, or do that is against God's way of living. Can you think of something you did today that was a sin? Let's each tell God about it and thank God for Jesus.

(Example: God, I'm sorry I was jealous of Tim's motorhome. Please help me be happy with what I have. Thank you, Jesus, for taking the punishment for my sin. I love You. Amen.)

Materials:
- embroidery needles
- stuffing
- scissors
- felt in red, green, and white/cream
- embroidery floss in red, green, black, and white/cream

How to Make:
- APPLE SKIN: cut out two apple skins from the red felt (one for the back and one for the front of the ornament).
- APPLE CORE: cut out the apple core from the white/cream felt. **TIP**: if you want an exactly-symmetrical apple, fold the felt in half and trace half a core, and then cut it out still folded. Once cut out, stitch two or three overlapping stitches in black to make apple seeds in the center of the apple. Using white/cream floss, stitch the core onto the front of a red apple skin.
- LEAF: cut out a leaf from the green felt, and sew onto the top of the red felt in the appropriate place.
- ATTACHING FRONT TO BACK: blanket stitch the two apple skins together, hiding the stitch behind the leaf as you stitch around the apple. Be sure to add some stuffing just before you sew it closed!

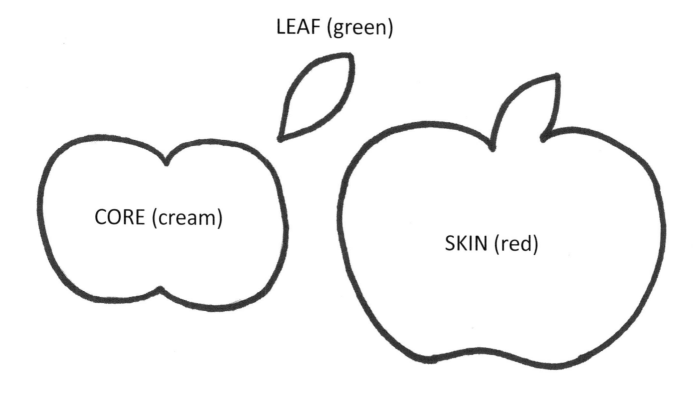

LEAF (green)

CORE (cream)

SKIN (red)

DAY 3 : Noah's Ark

Opening Activity: Get a CD and a flashlight. Put the CD upside down on your table or near a wall. Turn off the lights and shine the flashlight on the CD so the light reflects off the CD and makes a rainbow on the wall. Say: Today we are going to read about the very first rainbow God made.

Reading: "Whenever the rainbow appears in the clouds, I will see it and remember the everlasting covenant between God and all living creatures of every kind on the earth." (Genesis 6:11-14,18-22; 7:24-8:1; 9:11-16 or the story of Noah)

Symbol: Ark and Rainbow (sign of the covenant)

Summary: The descendants of Adam and Eve continued to disobey God, doing things their way and not the way God intended. God chose Noah and his family (a family that obeyed His law) and instructed them to build an ark. He then flooded the earth, which gave humankind a chance to start again through Noah's family. The rainbow was God's covenant; it's a promise that He will not flood the earth again.

Jesus Connection: How did God judge all the people on the earth? *(By sending a flood.)* What was the only way Noah, his family, and the animals could be saved from the flood? *(By getting on the ark.)* Just like the ark was the only way to be saved from God's judgement of the flood, Jesus is our only way to be saved from God's judgment of our sins. Noah's family had to enter through the door of the ark. Jesus is the door to heaven. In John 10:9, He said, "I am the door, by Me, if any man enter in, he shall be saved."

Prayer: Let's thank Jesus for taking the punishment for our sins. (Example: Thank You, Jesus, for dying on the cross for me and for being the doorway for me to enter heaven. I love You. Amen.)

DAY 3 : Noah's Ark

Materials:

- embroidery needles
- stuffing
- scissors
- felt in red, orange, yellow, green, blue, white, gray, tan, and brown
- embroidery floss in red, orange, yellow, green, blue, white, gray, tan, and black and brown

See page 6 for photo of ornament

How to Make:

- BACKGROUND: cut out two background pieces from red felt (one for the back and one for the front of the ornament).
- RAINBOW: cut out the arcs. Starting with the orange felt, sew the orange arc to the red background with orange floss. Next, sew the yellow felt in place, stitching through both the red and orange felt; the arcs should overlap. Repeat with green and blue felt, always using matching color floss.
- CLOUD: cut out the cloud from white felt, and position so the cloud overlaps each of the arcs of the rainbow, ensuring each color in the rainbow tucks underneath the cloud. Stitch the cloud with white floss onto the red base, sewing through the rainbow arcs which fit nicely under the cloud.
- ELEPHANT: stitch an eye on the elephant by making a French knot with black floss. Then, position the elephant's body on the rainbow and stitch in place with gray floss. Lay the ear over the elephant's body, and stitch in place.
- LION: lay the tan head onto the brown mane. Sew two eyes and a nose by making French knots with brown floss – these should go through both the tan and brown felt as this attaches them together. Add in a little backstitched lion smile. Stitch the lion's mane to the red felt base, overlapping the rainbow arcs.
- ARK: sew the blue waves to the ark with blue floss, then sew the ark onto the red base. The arc should overlap the elephant, lion, and parts of the rainbow.
- ATTACHING FRONT TO BACK: backstitch the two red felt pieces together, sneaking a few stitches underneath the cloud, ark, and lion so the red doesn't show on the front of your ornament. Be sure to add some stuffing just before you sew it closed!

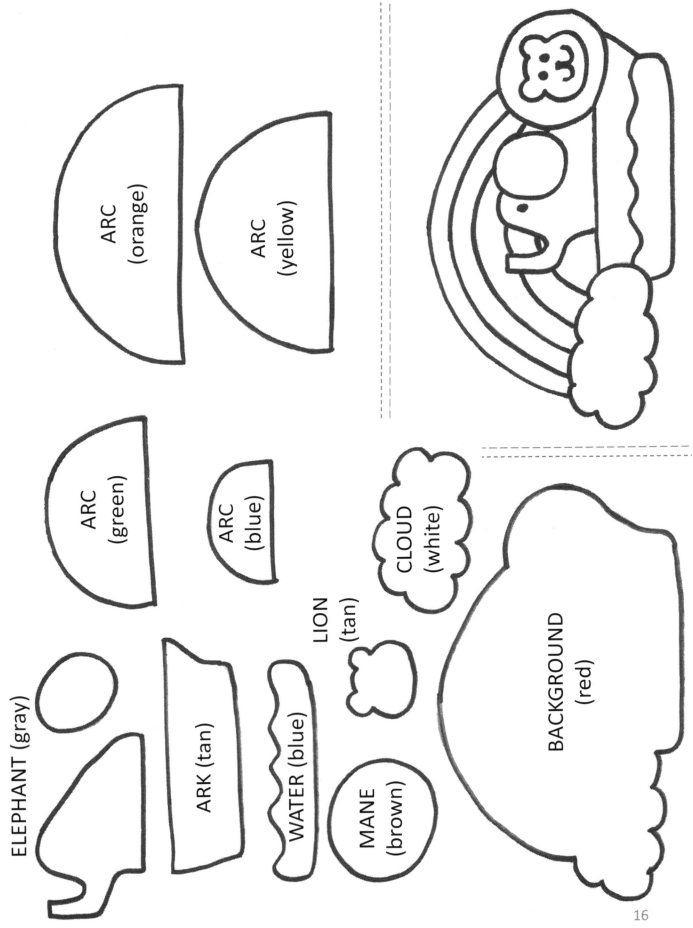

ARC (orange)

ARC (yellow)

ARC (green)

ARC (blue)

CLOUD (white)

LION (tan)

ELEPHANT (gray)

ARK (tan)

WATER (blue)

MANE (brown)

BACKGROUND (red)

16

DAY 4: Tower of Babel

Opening Activity: With your children, build as tall of a tower as you can using blocks, plastic cups, Legos, or whatever materials you have on hand. Say: Today we are going to learn about a group of people who tried to build a tower that went all the way to heaven.

Reading: "Then they said, "Come, let us build ourselves a city, with a tower that reaches to the heavens, so that we may make a name for ourselves; otherwise we will be scattered over the face of the whole earth." (Genesis 11:1-9 or the story of the Tower of Babel)

Symbol: Tower

Summary: God's people continued to struggle in obeying God and following his rule. One group chose to live apart from God, and built a great tower so they could "make a name for themselves". God saw that they were constructing not only a tower but a life apart from Him. He made it so the people no longer all spoke the same language; as they could not clearly communicate with each other, the tower was never completed. God stopped the people from further separating themselves from Him.

Jesus Connection: After the flood, God told the people to spread out. But the people disobeyed. They stayed together and tried to build a tower all the way to heaven, but nobody can build a tower to heaven. There is only one way to get to heaven, and that is through Jesus, God's Son. God scattered the people because they were not obeying Him and because they were building the tower for themselves, not for God. Now we have many groups of people who speak different languages and are part of different nations. One day, God will gather together everyone who believes in Jesus from every nation, and we will all be together again praising God in heaven.

Prayer: Let's thank Jesus for providing a way to heaven. (Example: Thank You, Jesus, for making a way for people of all nations to be saved. It will be pretty amazing seeing people from all over the world together worshipping you in heaven. I love You. Amen.

DAY 4: Tower of Babel

Materials:
- embroidery needles
- stuffing
- scissors
- felt in blue, gray, green, and white
- embroidery floss in blue, gray, green, and white

How to Make:
- BACKGROUND: cut out two rectangles from the blue felt (one for the back and one for the front of the ornament).
- TOWER: cut out the four trapezoids from the gray felt. Stack them on an angle to form the tower. Once you like the placement, sew the pieces down to blue felt, sewing the top piece first and working your way down. They should slightly overlap.
- CLOUDS: cut out two small white clouds and stitch them down around the top of the tower. The tower extended up towards the heavens, so we want to show this is a tall tower!
- GRASS: cut out the strip of green felt and sew it along the base of the rectangle.
- ATTACHING FRONT TO BACK: blanket stitch the two pieces of blue felt together. Be sure to add some stuffing just before you sew it closed!

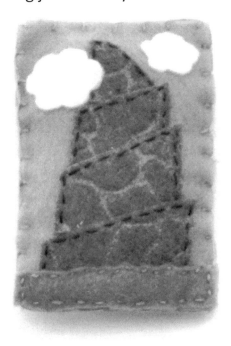

- -

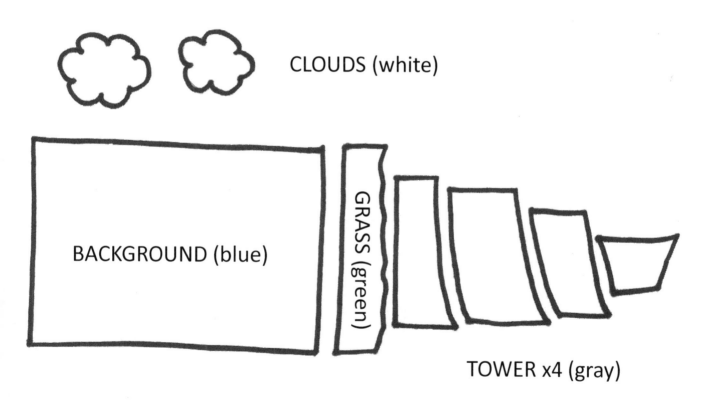

CLOUDS (white)

BACKGROUND (blue)

GRASS (green)

TOWER x4 (gray)

DAY 5 : Abraham/Stars

Opening Activity: Take your children outside and look up at the stars. There are so many! Try to count how many stars there are. Tell them there are many more stars that are too far away to see.

Reading: ""Look up at the sky and count the stars—if indeed you can count them." Then he said to him, "So shall your offspring be."" (Genesis 15:1-6 or the story of God's promise to Abraham)

Symbol: Sky full of stars (descendants of Abraham)

Summary: Abraham and Sarah obeyed, believed, and trusted God – even when things seemed at their darkest. God, in turn, promised Abraham that he would be blessed and that his descendants would be as many as the stars in the sky.

Jesus Connection: God told Abraham that He would give him a family that would be too big to count. Abraham did have a son who had many children, who then had many children, who then had many children, and so on. But there is a secret message. God had a different family in mind. Galatians 3:7 says "it is those who are of faith who are sons of Abraham." That means that anyone who believes in Jesus is part of the promise God made Abraham. We are part of the family that is like the stars—too big to count.

Prayer: Let's thank Jesus for making a way for us to be part of God's family. (Example: Thank You, Jesus for making me part of Your family. Please teach me what it means to live as God's child. I love You. Amen.)

DAY 5 : Abraham/Stars

Materials:
- embroidery needles
- stuffing
- scissors
- felt in blue and two shades of green
- embroidery floss in blue and green
- glittery metallic gold thread
- background music: Father Abraham Had Many Sons

How to Make:
- BACKGROUND: cut out two background pieces from the blue felt (one for the back and one for the front of the ornament).
- HILLSIDE: cut out a strip of hillside from the darker green felt and stitch using the green floss to the sky/background.
- GRASSES: cut out the grasses from the lighter green felt and stitch down on top of the existing hillside. You'll need to sew through three layers of felt, as you are attaching the green grasses to not only the hillside but the background sky as well.
- STARS: to make the stars, sew randomly-arranged French knots onto your sky using sparkly gold thread. (Be careful...it tends to tangle.)
- ATTACHING FRONT TO BACK: blanket stitch the two rectangles together. Be sure to add some stuffing just before you sew it closed!

FAITH and Fabric

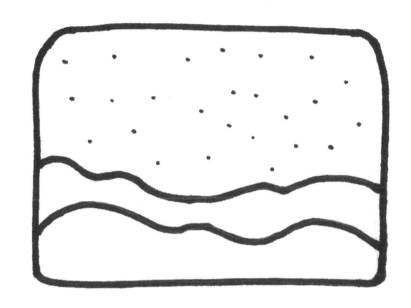

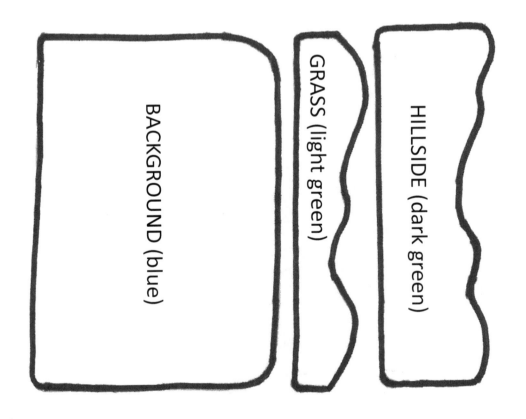

BACKGROUND (blue)

GRASS (light green)

HILLSIDE (dark green)

DAY 6 : Isaac/Ram

Opening Activity: Have your children stand with arms to their sides. Stand behind them and ask them to fall straight backwards without bending their knees or moving their arms to catch themselves. Your children need to trust you to catch them. Say: Was it hard for you to trust that I would catch you? Today, we are going to learn about a time where it was SUPER hard for Abraham to trust in God.

Reading: "Abraham looked up and there in a thicket he saw a ram caught by its horns. He went over and took the ram and sacrificed it as a burnt offering instead of his son." (Genesis 22:1-18 or the story of Abraham sacrificing Isaac)

Symbol: Ram in brush

Summary: God's promise to Abraham and Sarah was kept in the birth of their son Isaac. God wanted to ensure that Abraham was still obedient to Him, so he ordered Abraham to sacrifice his son, Isaac. Abraham trusted and obeyed God, and showed his faith in his works by doing as he is told. God sent a message – at the last moment – to Abraham instructing him to not kill his son, and provided a ram to be used as a sacrifice in place of Isaac. Abraham showed his complete trust in God.

Jesus Connection: It might seem strange that God asked Abraham to sacrifice his only son, but God had a plan to use this story to give Israel, God's people, a hint about Jesus. Jesus is like Isaac in this story. Just like Abraham was supposed to sacrifice his one and only son, God sacrificed His one and only Son, Jesus. But unlike Isaac, God didn't have a ram take Jesus' place. Jesus is also like the ram in this story. God gave Abraham the ram to take the place of Isaac. God gives Jesus to take our place. We all deserve death, to be separated from God here on earth and forever after we die. But if we believe Jesus died to take the punishment for our sins and then rose again, we can have eternal life—knowing God here on earth and forever with Him in heaven.

Prayer: Let's thank God for sending Jesus to take the punishment for our sins. (Example: God, I know I deserve punishment since I sin against You. Thank You for sending Jesus to take my place. Help me be like Abraham and live out my faith by trusting and serving You. I love You, Amen.)

DAY 6: Isaac/Ram

Materials:
- embroidery needles
- stuffing
- scissors
- felt in tan, cream, and green
- embroidery floss in tan, dark brown, cream, and green

How to Make:
- RAM: cut two rams from the cream felt (one for the back and one for the front of the ornament).
- HORNS: cut out the horns from the tan felt, ensuring it fits neatly fit onto the cream colored part of the ram. You will attach with a basic front stitch...but not yet.
- TANGLED BRUSH: cut the random jagged "brush" pattern out of the green felt. Lay it over the cream colored ram body and "tangle" it into the ram's still-unattached horn. One you like the tangle, sew both the horns and the brush onto the ram.
- FACE: back stitch, in dark brown, a mouth and triangular nose. Make an eye (or two) with a French knot.
- ATTACHING FRONT TO BACK: blanket stitch the two cream felt pieces together. You'll have to sneak a few stitches underneath the horns and brush. Be sure to add some stuffing just before you sew it closed!

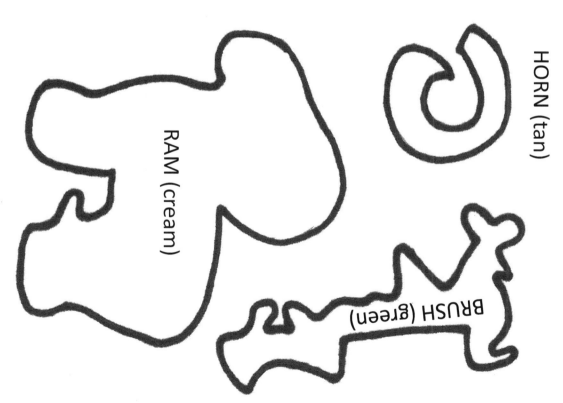

RAM (cream)

HORN (tan)

BRUSH (green)

FAITH
and
Fabric

DAY 7: Jacob/Ladder

Opening Activity: Have everyone in the family take turns sharing about a crazy dream they have had.

Reading: "And he dreamed, and behold, there was a ladder set up on the earth, and the top of it reached to heaven. And behold, the angels of God were ascending and descending on it!" (Genesis 28:10-22 or the story of Jacob's dream)

Symbol: Ladder reaching into the heavens

Summary: Jacob, son of Isaac and Rebekah, had a twin brother Esau. Jacob and Esau quarreled with each other even in Rebekah's womb, and it continued in childhood and young adult years. Jacob received a blessing from his father that should have gone to his brother Esau (by birthright), and left the city. He stoped on his departure for the night, and had a dream of a stairway/ladder that went from the ground up into the heavens. Upon the ladder are God's messengers, and God told Jacob that he is blessed and his descendants will be as plentiful as the dust of the earth. It is validation that Jacob should indeed have received the blessing from his father.

Jesus Connection: Where did the ladder in Jacob's dream go? (*To heaven*) Who was going up and down the ladder? *(Angels)* Jacob's dream is another secret message for us. In John 1:51, Jesus refers to this story and says that He is the ladder to heaven! In John 14:6, Jesus said, "I am the way, the truth, and the life, no one comes to the Father but by Me."

Prayer: Let's thank Jesus for making a way for us know God and live with Him forever. (Example: Thank You, Jesus, for being the way to heaven. Now I can know God and live for Him. I love You. Amen.)

DAY 7 : Jacob/Ladder

Materials:
- embroidery needles
- stuffing
- scissors
- felt in blue, white, and brown
- embroidery floss in white and brown

How to Make:
- SKY: cut out two background pieces from the blue felt (one for the back and one for the front of the ornament).
- CLOUDS: cut out the two clouds, one smaller than the other, from the white felt. Set aside.
- LADDER: cut out the ladder from the brown felt and set aside.
- COMBINING PIECES: arrange the clouds and ladder on one piece of the blue felt, placing one cloud (the larger one) behind the ladder. Once you like the arrangement, begin stitching them down: using white floss, stitch the larger cloud onto one of the pieces of blue felt. Next, using brown floss, stitch the ladder onto the blue felt overlapping some of the larger white cloud. Then, place the smaller white cloud in the upper left corner and stitch it on top of the ladder.
- ATTACHING FRONT TO BACK: blanket stitch the sky/background pieces together. Be sure to add some stuffing just before you sew it closed!

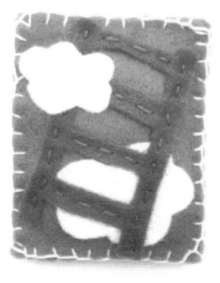

FAITH and Fabric

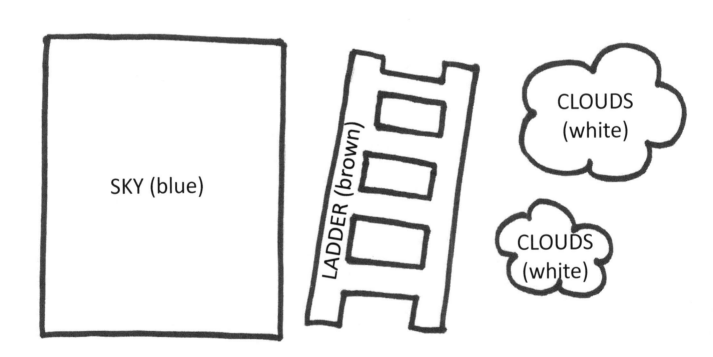

SKY (blue)

LADDER (brown)

CLOUDS (white)

CLOUDS (white)

DAY 8: Joseph/Coat

Opening Activity: Get a toy person (Lego figure, Little People, action figure, etc.) and a container large enough to hold the toy person. Have your children stand next to the container and toss the toy person into the container. Make it harder by trying to toss the figure into the container from a farther distance. Say: In our story today, some men threw their brother in a pit. Let's read and find out what happens.

Reading: "Now Israel loved Joseph more than any of his other sons, because he had been born to him in his old age; and he made an ornate robe for him." (Genesis 37:1-4, 12-28; 41:1-41; 42:1-2; and 45:1-11 or the story of Joseph)

Symbol: Joseph's robe (often known as the coat of many colors)

Summary: Joseph, the beloved son of Jacob, was the envy of his brothers. While Jacob loved all his children, Joseph held a special place in his heart. Their jealousy of the relationship between him and their father reached a peak when Joseph appeared in an ornate coat (a gift from their father). They threw him into a pit, sold him into slavery, only to – years later – meet up with him again in Egypt. Through trust in God, Joseph eventually thrived in Egypt and not only reconciled but has his family migrate to Egypt once they reconnect.

Jesus Connection: Joseph's brothers hated him. He was sold into slavery, punished even though he did no wrong, and then ended up saving his people from a terrible famine. Even though there was a lot of bad things that happened in Joseph's life, God used it for good. The story of Joseph is a little hint of the story of Jesus. Jesus left His heavenly home with God the Father. Jesus was hated, sold for pieces of silver, punished even though He did no wrong, and saves His people from God's judgment. Even though dying on the cross seems a very bad thing that happened to Jesus, it was part of God's plan for good—to save us from the punishment of our sins and bring us into a right relationship with God.

Prayer: Let's thank God for taking the bad and using it for good. (Example: Thank You, God, that no matter how bad life gets, You promise to use it for the good of making me like You. And thank You for having the good plan of salvation.)

FAITH
and
Fabric

DAY 8: Joseph/Coat

Materials:
- embroidery needles
- stuffing
- scissors
- scraps of felt in lots of colors!
- embroidery floss lots of colors!

How to Make:
- COAT: this ornament is a great way to use up the scraps you have! First, cut out two coats from a piece of felt; any color will work (one for the back and one for the front of the ornament).
- UNDERGARMENT: cut out the strip of white to represent the undergarments that Joseph would be wearing. It is the length of the coat; place in the center and stitch it down with white floss.
- COAT COLORS: using any scrap color pieces you want, in any combination you want, attach patches of color to the coat. Remember, this is the coat of MANY colors so have fun with it!
- ATTACHING FRONT TO BACK: blanket stitch the two pieces together. Be sure to add some stuffing just before you sew it closed!

COAT
(any color)

UNDERGARMENTS
(white)

DAY 9: Moses/Burning Bush

Opening Activity: Hide somewhere in your house and call your kids by name so they have to find you by following your voice. Say: In today's Bible story, we are going to read about a man who had God calling his name from a burning bush.

Reading: "There the angel of the Lord appeared to him in flames of fire from within a bush. Moses saw that though the bush was on fire it did not burn up." (Exodus 3:1-15 or the story of Moses and the Burning Bush)

Symbol: Burning bush

Summary: God's people drifted away from Him, and He chose Moses to lead His chosen people out from Egyptian rule. Moses, born to God's people but raised by Pharaoh's daughter, was in the unique position to understand both cultures. One day, God called Moses, speaking to him through a burning bush. Moses trusted God and brought God's people out from Egyptian rule so the people could worship God and live the way He intended.

Jesus Connection: God sent Moses to free His people from slavery in Egypt and bring them to the Promised Land. The story of Moses is a clue God gave Israel to tell them about Jesus. One day God would send His Son to free His people from the slavery of sin and bring them into the promise of eternal life.

Prayer: Let's thank God for giving us clues in the Bible that point to Jesus and for sending Jesus to free us from our slavery to sin. (Example: Thank You, God, for giving so many secret messages about Jesus so many years before He was born. Just like the Israelites were slaves, I was a slave to my sin. Thank You for sending Jesus to set me free. I love You. Amen)

DAY 9: Moses/Burning Bush

Materials:
- embroidery needles
- stuffing
- scissors
- felt in green, yellow, brown, and red
- embroidery floss in green, yellow, brown, and red

How to Make:
- BACKGROUND: cut out two bushes from the green felt (one for the back and one for the front of the ornament).
- BRANCHES: cut out the branches / base of the bush out of brown felt; this will represent the bottom stem and a few lower branches. Once you cut the branches, sew it onto the background / green felt.
- RED AND YELLOW FLAMES: cut out the larger set of flames from the red felt. Sew it down on top of the brown felt, making sure you see the bottom of the brown felt branches below the flame. Do the same with the yellow flames.
- ATTACHING FRONT TO BACK: blanket stitch the two pieces together. Be sure to add some stuffing just before you sew it closed!

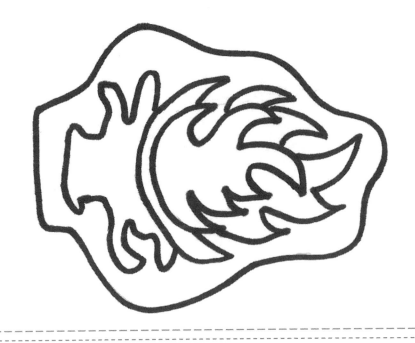

FLAMES
(yellow)

FLAMES
(red)

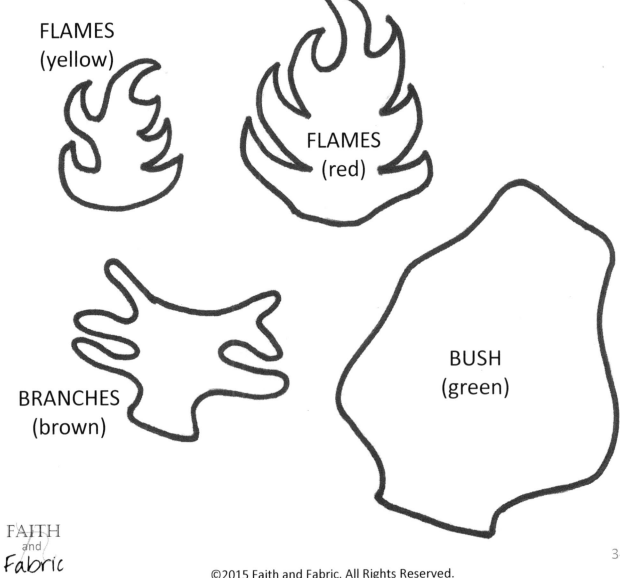

BRANCHES
(brown)

BUSH
(green)

DAY 10: Ten Commandments

Opening Activity: Have your kids line up and play red light, green light. When you say green light, they can move forward toward you. When you say red light they need to stop. When they get to you, give them a high five. Say: When we drive our cars, we have to obey the rules of the road. The rules help keep us safe. Today, we're going to read about God giving His people rules to follow.

Reading: "The Lord said to Moses, "Come up to me on the mountain and stay here, and I will give you the tablets of stone with the law and commandments I have written for their instruction."" (Exodus 19-20, 24:12 or the story of the Ten Commandments)

Symbol: Two tablets containing the written ten commandments.

Summary: God, once his people were out from Egyptian rule, began to guide His people and taught them how He wanted them to live. He created a new covenant with them through the Ten Commandments, given to Moses on Mount Sinai.

Jesus Connection: Paul tells us in Romans 7:7 that God's law teaches us what sin is. God gave us the law so we would realize that we are all sinners because we can't ever keep God's laws perfectly. The law shows God's people that they need a Savior. We now know that the Savior is Jesus Christ. Only Jesus lived a perfect life, not breaking any of God's commandments. He rescued us from our sins, takes our punishment, and gives us His perfection as Lord and Savior. Now that we have Christ's perfection in God's eyes, we can live each day striving to turn away from sin and live more and more like Christ.

Prayer: Can you think of something you did today that was a sin and broke a commandment? Let's each tell God about it and thank God for Jesus, and think of a way we could keep that commandment next time. (Example: Dear God, I'm sorry I fought with my sister over our toys today. I want to love her the way You love me. Thank You, Jesus, for forgiving me. I love you. Amen.)

DAY 10: Ten Commandments

Materials:
- embroidery needles
- stuffing
- scissors
- felt in black and gray
- embroidery floss in black and gray

How to Make:
- BACKGROUND and TABLET: cut out two of the large background pieces from black felt (one for the back and one for the front of the ornament). Set aside. Cut out one smaller tablet from gray felt.
- NUMBERING: this is slightly tricky. Start in the middle (with the third Roman numeral) so it is centered on the tablet, then sew the two Roman numerals above and two below. Repeat for the other side. Use the black floss so the numerals stand out.
- BACKGROUND: sew the gray tablet - with gray floss – to the piece of black felt. Stitch the center of the tablets down as well using the same color floss, so it looks more like two distinct tablets.
- ATTACHING FRONT TO BACK: blanket stitch the two black pieces together. Be sure to add some stuffing just before you sew it closed!

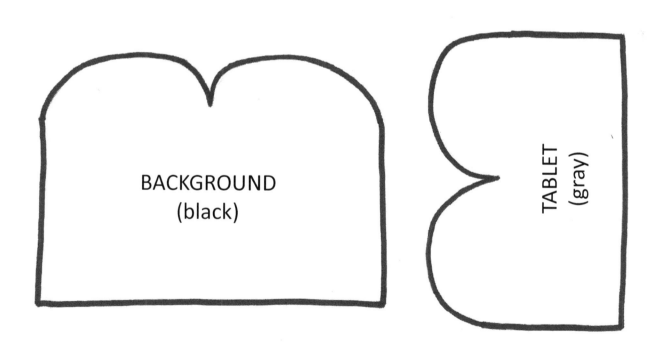

BACKGROUND
(black)

TABLET
(gray)

DAY 11 : Joshua & Rahab

Opening Activity: Play the game I Spy with your children. Spot something in the room and say, "I spy with my little eye something....*(the color of the object.)*" Your children guess what it is that you spy. At the end of the game, say: In our Bible story today, we are going to learn about two spies who almost got caught! Let's see what happens.

Reading: "So she let them down by a rope through the window, for the house she lived in was part of the city wall." (Joshua 1:1-9; 2:1-21; 6:1-25 or the stories of Rahab and the Spies and the Battle of Jericho)

Symbol: Wall of Jericho with Rahab's rope hanging over the wall, through which God's spies climbed into the city.

Summary: Both Joshua and Rahab showed complete trust in God! Joshua could not have broken into the city of Jericho without God's divine promise of assistance. Rahab came as the unlikely answer to God's promise; a woman who lived in the walls of Jericho who trusted and believed in the God of Abraham. Rahab kept two of Joshua's spies safe and, in return, they promised to keep her and her family safe during the siege. She tied a scarlet rope on her window so God's people would know which home was hers, thereby identifying her so they could protect her. For both Joshua and Rahab, their trust and obedience to God kept them and their families safe and free.

Jesus Connection: What color cord did Rahab need to hang out her window in order to be saved when the Israelites fought the city of Jericho? *(Red/scarlet)* The red cord is a little clue pointing to Jesus. Just like Rahab needed the red cord to save her from the battle, we need the red blood that Jesus shed on the cross to save us from our sins.

Fun Fact: Rahab is the great, great, great, far off grandma to Jesus! (Matthew 1:5)

Prayer: Let's thank God for saving Rahab and thank Jesus for dying to save us! (Example: Thank You, God, for saving Rahab so many years ago. And thank You for saving me. I love You. Amen.)

FAITH
and
Fabric

DAY 11 : Joshua & Rahab

Materials:

- embroidery needles
- stuffing
- scissors
- ribbon or rope in red
- felt in tan/brown
- embroidery floss in brown
- background music: Joshua Fought the Battle of Jericho

How to Make:

- BACKGROUND: cut out two rectangles (walls) from the tan felt (one for the back and one for the front of the ornament).
- BRICKS: stitch bricks into one of the background (wall) pieces. They should be random and not exactly even...bricks today are not what bricks were so long ago.
- ROPE: cut a red rope the length of the background (wall). Knot one end of the rope. Sew the other end to the inside of the wall at the top.
- ATTACHING FRONT TO BACK: starting at the top, blanket stitch the two walls pieces together. Be sure to add some stuffing just before you sew it closed!

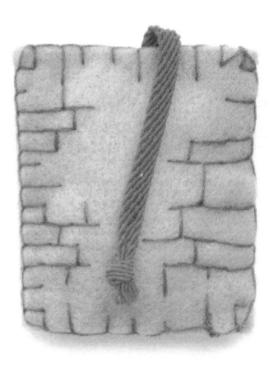

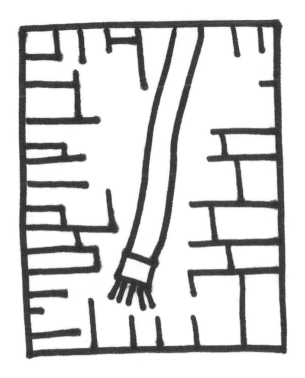

BACKGROUND
(tan)

DAY 12: Naomi & Ruth

Opening Activity: Play the game Follow the Leader. Pick one person to be the leader. The leader can move or do any action, and the rest of the family needs to copy what the leader does. Say: In our Bible story today, we learn about a lady who follows her mother-in-law to a far away land.

Reading: "So Ruth stayed close to the women of Boaz to glean until the barley and wheat harvests were finished." (Ruth 1-4 or the story of Ruth)

Symbol: Stalks of barley collected by Ruth

Summary: Ruth, born to a family who did not accept God, married into a family that does; she came to know God and accepted Him. When her husband died, she chose to stay with her mother-in-law, Naomi: "wherever you go, I go, wherever you lodge, I lodge, your people shall be my people, and your God my God." Ruth cared for Naomi, and worked in the fields of Naomi's extended kin, Boaz. God established a place for Naomi and Ruth, and Boaz married Ruth. Ruth gave birth to a son, named Obed. Obed becomes the father of Jesse, who becomes the father of David.

Jesus Connection: Today, women can work and provide for their families if they don't have a husband or dad. But back when Ruth and Naomi were alive, it was a lot harder for women. So God had special rules in place to help women who didn't have a dad, husband, or son. A close relative was able to do a special job called a kinsman redeemer. As Ruth's kinsman redeemer, Boaz promised to pay for the land that used to belong to Ruth's husband. He also promised to marry Ruth and take care of Ruth and her mother-in-law, Naomi, for the rest of their lives. Boaz was a special picture to teach us about Jesus. The Bible calls Jesus our redeemer. He pays the price for our sins and promises to care for us forever.

Fun Fact: Just like Rahab, Ruth is another great, great, great, far off grandma to Jesus! (Matthew 1:5)

Prayer: Let's thank Jesus for being our redeemer, paying the price of our sins and taking care of us. (Example: Dear Jesus, thank You for being my redeemer. Thank You for paying the price of my sins and choosing to care for me. I love You. Amen.)

DAY 12: Naomi & Ruth

Materials:
- embroidery needles
- stuffing
- scissors
- felt in tan and green
- embroidery floss in brown and green

How to Make:
- BACKGROUND: cut out two ovals from the green felt (one for the back and one for the front of the ornament).
- WHEAT: cut out the thin zig-zag wheat stalks from the tan felt. Repeat two more times...and remember, they should look organic, not the same. Sew the three wheat strands onto one of the green felt ovals. Sew the outside two strands, then sew the middle down so it overlaps a bit on the other two strands of wheat. To sew, stitch a simple stitch up the stem from the top to the bottom, leaving the actual side strands of wheat unattached.
- ATTACHING FRONT TO BACK: blanket stitch the two background pieces together. Be sure to add some stuffing just before you sew it closed!

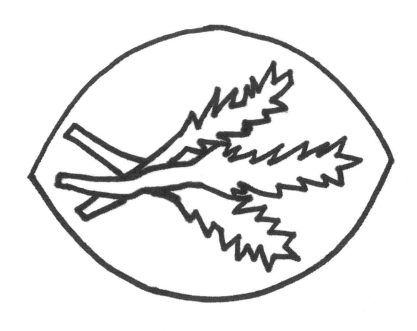

- -

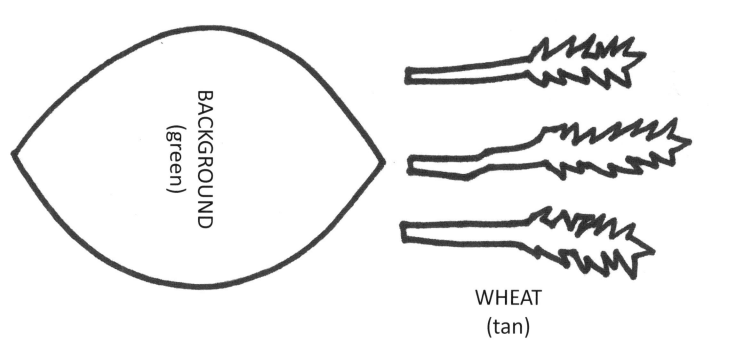

BACKGROUND
(green)

WHEAT
(tan)

DAY 13: Samuel/Oil Lamp

Opening Activity: Collect items that make noise, such as a hammer, timer, paper crinkling, pen clicking, or a noisy toy. Put them all in a pillow case so your children can't see them. Reach into the pillow case and cause one of the items to make a noise. After each item makes it's noise, have your children guess what the object is. Show them the object so they know if they guessed correctly. Say: In our story today, we are reading about a boy who heard something strange.

Reading: "The lamp of God had not yet gone out, and Samuel was lying down in the house of the Lord, where the ark of God was. The Lord called to Samuel, who answered, "Here I am."" (1 Samuel 2:26-3:21 or the story of Samuel)

Symbol: Samuel's oil lamp.

Summary: Samuel grew up in the services of the Lord, under Eli. One day, Eli was asleep and Samuel heard a voice call his name. He went to Eli, but Eli said he did not call him. This happened twice more; the third time he was called, Samuel responded with, "Speak, for your servant is listening." Samuel was open to and received God's message.

Jesus Connection: Samuel was being raised by Eli the priest. In the Old Testament, a priest would sacrifice the animals to cover the sins of the people. Before God talked to Samuel, He sent a messenger to talk to Eli. God was no longer going let Eli's family be priests because Eli and his sons were disobedient to God. The messenger also said that God was going to raise up a faithful priest who would serve Him always (1 Samuel 2:35). While Samuel did grow up to be a faithful priest, Samuel - and every person - eventually dies. Therefore, God was giving a clue about Someone else! Who do you think this is? *(Jesus!)* Hebrews 4:14-16 tells us why it is so amazing that Jesus is our High Priest. "Therefore, since we have a great high priest who has ascended into heaven, Jesus the Son of God, let us hold firmly to the faith we profess. For we do not have a high priest who is unable to empathize with our weaknesses, but we have one who has been tempted in every way, just as we are—yet He did not sin. Let us then approach God's throne of grace with confidence, so that we may receive mercy and find grace to help us in our time of need." Because Jesus is our High Priest, we have confidence, comfort and grace.

FAITH
and
Fabric

DAY 13: Samuel/Oil Lamp

Prayer: Let's thank Jesus for being our High Priest and thank God for giving us the opportunity to hear them and serve. (Example: Thank You, Jesus, being my High Priest and for calling me to serve! You make it so I can know God forever!)

Fun Fact: Samuel and Jesus are similar in another way. 1 Samuel 2:26 says, "And the boy Samuel continued to grow in stature and in favor with the Lord and with people." Luke 2:52 says, "And Jesus grew in wisdom and stature, and in favor with God and man."

Materials:
- embroidery needles
- stuffing
- scissors
- felt in black, gray, red, and yellow
- embroidery floss in black, gray, red, and yellow

How to Make:
- BACKGROUND: cut out two rectangles from the black felt (one for the back and one for the front of the ornament).
- LAMP: cut out the lamp-shaped figure from the gray felt and stitch down onto the black rectangle. Next, cut out a red flame and stitch that above the lamp. Cut out the yellow flame, and stitch it on top of the red.
- ATTACHING FRONT TO BACK: blanket stitch the two black rectangles together. Be sure to add some stuffing just before you sew it closed!

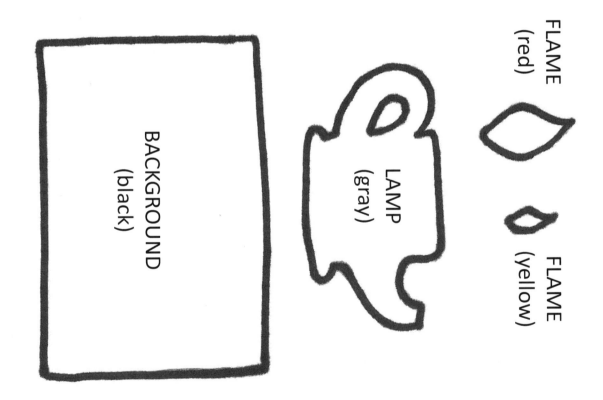

BACKGROUND
(black)

LAMP
(gray)

FLAME
(red)

FLAME
(yellow)

DAY 14: Jesse/Shepherd

Opening Activity: Before your devotion time, pick two items from your pantry, one that is appealing to kids, like a box of cookies, and one that they would never pick to eat, like a box of tea bags. Take the appealing food out of it's box and put it in the box of the unappealing food. Put the unappealing food in the appealing food box. Bring the two boxes out to the kids and ask them to pick which one they would like to eat for snack/dessert. After they realize they've been tricked, let them eat the appealing snack and say: In today's Bible story, we're going to read about how God makes His choice based on who someone is on the inside, not what he looks like on the outside.

Reading: "Jesse had seven of his sons pass before Samuel, but Samuel said to him, "The Lord has not chosen these."" (1 Samuel 16 or the story of Jesse)

Symbol: Sheep and eight flowers. Jesse was a shepherd, so this ornament shows the sheep to which he tended. Below the sheep are eight flowers; seven in red, representing the seven sons that the Lord did not choose, and an eighth in yellow, for David, whom the Lord did choose.

Summary: God's people wanted a king, and Saul was selected. Saul didn't follow God's direction, so God sent Samuel to the house of Jesse to find the next king. God guided Samuel to make David, the youngest and smallest son of Jesse, the chosen king.

Jesus Connection: Even though Jesse doesn't seem like the most important person in this Bible story, he is part of an important clue that God gives His people. Jesse was the dad of David, who was chosen to be king because God looked at the inside of his heart. God saw inside David and knew he was a man after God's own heart. Isaiah 11 tells us of a another King who will come from Jesse's family. This will be a forever King; and "the Spirit of the Lord will rest on Him, the spirit of wisdom and understanding, the spirit of counsel and strength, the spirit of knowledge and the fear of the Lord. And He will delight in the fear of the Lord...The nations will resort to the root of Jesse, who will stand as a signal for the peoples; And His resting place will be glorious" (vs. 2-3a, 10). Do you know who this forever King is? *(Jesus!)*

Fun Fact: Jesse and David were great, great, far off grandpas to Jesus.

DAY 14: Jesse/Shepherd

Prayer: Let's thank Jesus for being our forever king. (Example: Thank You, Jesus, for being my forever King! Help me change my life so I am living for You instead of myself. I love You. Amen.)

Materials:
- embroidery needles
- stuffing
- scissors
- felt in green, white, and tan
- embroidery floss in black, green, white, tan, red, and yellow

How to Make:
- BACKGROUND: cut out two rectangles from the green felt (one for the back and one for the front of the ornament).
- SHEEP: first, cut out the two sheep pieces (body and head) from white felt. Cut out four small squares from the tan felt for the feet. Arrange them on the green felt, and sew them down in this order: feet, body of sheep, head of sheep.
- SHEEP DETAIL: for the face, sew three French knots: two in black for the eyes, and one in pink for the nose. Sew a straight stitch for the mouth just below the nose.
- FLOWERS: sew seven red flowers and one yellow; each is a French knot. Use whatever colors you want for your flower combo – just be sure to make seven of one color and one of another. **TIP**: avoid brown*
- ATTACHING FRONT TO BACK: blanket stitch the two background pieces together. Be sure to add some stuffing just before you sew it closed!

* have to share a story here. The first time I made this, I used brown and not red for the flowers. Hubby wanted to know why I made "sheep droppings" on the ornament. Boys. Out came the brown French knots and in went the red ones. For your purposes, use whatever colors you want for your flower combo – just not brown.

BACKGROUND
(green)

SHEEP
(white)

LEGS
(tan)

DAY 15 : David/Slingshot

Opening Activity: Go outside, get a stone, and make a target out of something (a bucket, a paper on the ground...). Take turns tossing the stone from different distances and see who can hit the target. Say: In our Bible story today, we are going to learn how God helped David have amazing aim with a stone.

Reading: "Then he took his staff in his hand, chose five smooth stones from the stream, put them in the pouch of his shepherd's bag and, with his sling in his hand, approached the Philistine." (1 Samuel 17 or the story of David and Goliath)

Symbol: David's slingshot, with which he defeated Goliath

Summary: David started out as a shepherd boy, and yet was chosen to lead God's people. Before he became a great king, he was filled with the Holy Spirit and fought a great giant who fought with the Philistines against the Israelites. God gave David courage and strength; David, in a single shot with his slingshot, killed Goliath. The Philistines retreated, and the Israelites were saved.

Jesus Connection: The Israelites were in great danger. Unless someone fought and won against the giant, Goliath, they would become servants to the Philistines. Goliath was such a fierce enemy and everybody was afraid to fight. God used the soon-to-be king David to bring victory to the Israelites. Like the Israelites, we are in a loosing battle. Our battle is against our sin and its punishment of death. We are unable to win the fight, but we have a King who went to battle for us. Jesus took the punishment for our sins, conquered death, and made a way for us to know God here on earth and forever in heaven.

Prayer: Let's thank Jesus for defeating sin. (Example: Thank You, Jesus, for defeating sin! I could never win without You. I love You. Amen.)

DAY 15 : David/Slingshot

Materials:
- embroidery needles
- stuffing
- scissors
- felt in gray, tan, and blue
- embroidery floss in black, tan, gray, and blue

How to Make:
- BACKGROUND: cut out two rectangles from the blue felt (one for the back and one for the front of the ornament).
- DAVID'S SLINGSHOT (Part 1): cut out the "Y" shaped slingshot from the tan. **NOTE:** the Bible says it's a sling David used, and not a slingshot. I went for the more recognizable slingshot shape; feel free to modify if you wish.
- STONES: cut out five stones from the gray felt. When cutting out, make sure they're rough looking and not perfect circles (remember, they're rocks). The Bible mentions five stones, so be sure to include all five of them.
- ATTACH TO BACKGROUND: place the "Y" on one of the blue felt rectangles, and arrange the stones. Sew the "Y" down with tan floss, and the stones down with gray floss.

- DAVID'S SLINGSHOT (Part 2): using the black floss, sew a French knot through the "Y" near the top. Then, push your needle through the "Y" right near the French knot you just made so your needle is now on the front of the felt. Insert the needle back through the top of the other "Y", leaving it slack so you can get the "sling" effect. Make a French knot on the second side.
- ATTACHING FRONT TO BACK: blanket stitch the two blue rectangles together. Be sure to add some stuffing just before you sew it closed!

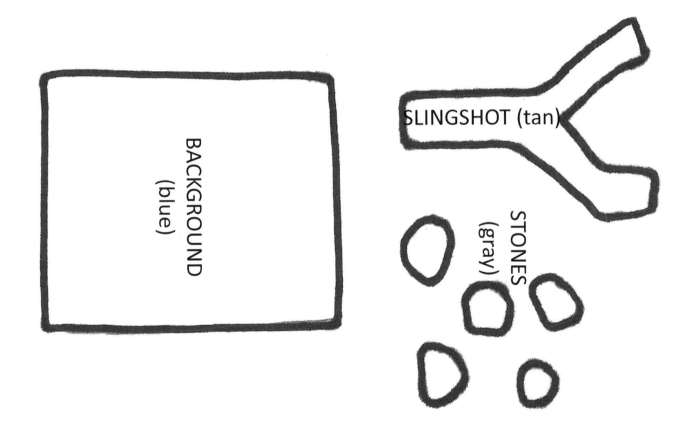

BACKGROUND
(blue)

SLINGSHOT (tan)

STONES
(gray)

DAY 16: Solomon/Temple

Opening Activity: Use blocks, Legos, Lincoln Logs, tupperware or whatever you have on hand to build a castle together. Say: In today's Bible story, we're going to learn about a king who made the most amazing building for God.

Reading: "The word of the LORD came to Solomon: "As for this temple you are building, if you follow my decrees, observe my laws and keep all my commands and obey them, I will fulfill through you the promise I gave to David your father. And I will live among the Israelites and will not abandon my people Israel." So Solomon built the temple and completed it." (1 Kings 6:11-14 or 2 Chronicles 1-7 (especially 2:1-16; 3:1-8; 5:11-14; 6:13-20 and 7:1-4) or the story of Solomon and the Temple)

Symbol: Solomon's temple

Summary: David was king for 40 years and, when he died, his son Solomon became king. Solomon's devout prayers to God to make him wise – knowing that wise kings made good decisions – were answered. God made Solomon the wisest king to lead His people. David continued to serve God and honor the covenant God made with His people.

Jesus Connection: Solomon was a wise and rich king who built an amazing temple for God. We have a forever King who is building an even better temple than what Solomon built. Who is our forever King? *(Jesus!)* People who believe in Jesus as their Lord and Savior receive God's grace and become part of the new Temple because God the Holy Spirit comes to live in them! 1 Corinthians 3:16 says, "Don't you know that you yourselves are God's temple and that God's Spirit dwells in your midst?"

Prayer: Let's thank God for living in us, loving us and helping us to be more like Him. (Example: Dear God, it is amazing that You live in me. Help me to be more like You. Thank You! I love You. Amen.)

FAITH and Fabric

DAY 16: Solomon/Temple

Materials:
- embroidery needles
- stuffing
- scissors
- felt in blue, green, tan, brown, and white
- embroidery floss in blue, green, tan, brown, gold, and white

How to Make:
- BACKGROUND: cut out two rectangles from the blue felt (one for the back and one for the front of the ornament).
- HILLS: cut out the green hills, and sew them down onto one of the blue felt rectangles with green floss.
- TEMPLE: cut out the temple from tan felt, and position on top of the green hills. Stitch down with tan floss. Cut out the door and two columns from the brown felt, and stitch down with brown floss. Embellish the temple with gold thread by making French knots along the top of the temple and between the two columns.
- CLOUDS: cut out the clouds from white felt, and sew into the sky on either side of the temple with white floss.
- ATTACHING FRONT TO BACK: blanket stitch the two blue rectangles together. Be sure to add some stuffing just before you sew it closed!

- -

CLOUDS
(white)

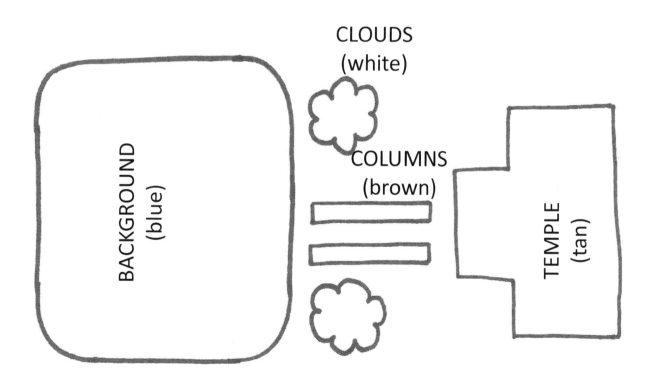

COLUMNS
(brown)

BACKGROUND
(blue)

TEMPLE
(tan)

DAY 17: Elijah/Stone Altar

Opening Activity: Take a paper towel and run it under water until it is **soaking** wet. Hold a lighter to it and show your kids how the paper towel won't catch fire because it is too full of water. (If you have an outdoor fire pit, you can also safely show them that when you hold the lighter up to a dry paper towel, it quickly catches fire and spreads.) Say: Today we're going to read about a time when God sent fire down from heaven, catching wood on fire even though it was soaking wet.

Reading: "At the time of sacrifice, the prophet Elijah stepped forward and prayed: "LORD, the God of Abraham, Isaac and Israel, let it be known today that you are God in Israel and that I am your servant and have done all these things at your command. Answer me, LORD, answer me, so these people will know that you, LORD, are God, and that you are turning their hearts back again." Then the fire of the LORD fell and burned up the sacrifice, the wood, the stones and the soil, and also licked up the water in the trench." (1 Kings 18 or the story of Elijah and the prophets of Baal)

Symbol: Stone altar with the fire of God burning the sacrifice

Summary: Many years after Solomon died, God's people were split into two kingdoms – Israel in the north and Judah in the south. Israel was under the rule of King Ahab - a king who did not follow God's law. God sent Elijah to bring His truth back to His people, who were under the influence of a leader who worshiped a different god. Elijah challenged the king's prophets to a test to prove that their god was not real. The king's prophets built one altar with a sacrifice, and Elijah built another with a sacrifice. The prophets called to their fake gods to send fire and burn the sacrifice, but nothing happens. Elijah called to God, and He sent fire that burned the offering. God showed His power to bring His people back to Him.

Jesus Connection: When Elijah was alive, the Israelites were disobeying God by not putting Him first in their lives. God used Elijah to save the Israelites from the sin of idolatry—which is worshipping anything other than God. Just like the Israelites, we do not always put God first in our lives. The Bible says putting other things before God is a sin. But we have a Savior, Jesus, who rescues us from our sins and welcomes us into God's kingdom of righteousness.

FAITH
and
Fabric

Our Family's Jesse Tree: Felt Ornaments v4
©2015 Faith and Fabric. All Rights Reserved.

56

DAY 17 : Elijah/Stone Altar

Prayer: Let's thank Jesus for rescuing us from a life trapped in sin. (Example: Thank You, Jesus, for rescuing us from a life trapped in sin. I'm sorry for making other things more important in my life. Please help me learn how keep You/God as most important. I love You. Amen.)

Materials:
- embroidery needles
- stuffing
- scissors
- felt in tan, gray, red, and yellow
- embroidery floss in tan, gray, red, and yellow

How to Make:
- BACKGROUND: cut out two background shapes from the tan felt (one for the back and one for the front of the ornament).
- STONES: cut out the stones from the gray felt. Remember, these are stones so be sure to keep some edges flat and jagged (they're not perfect circles). If you want to display exactly 12 stones (the Bible says there were 12 stones, one for each of the tribes of Israel), feel free!
- FIRE: cut out the larger flames from the red felt and the smaller flames from the yellow felt. Position the red flames over the top of the stones and stitch down with red floss. Position the yellow flames at the base of the red flames and stitch down with yellow floss.
- ATTACHING FRONT TO BACK: blanket stitch the two tan background shapes together. Be sure to add some stuffing just before you sew it closed!

BACKGROUND
(tan)

FIRE
(yellow)

FIRE
(red)

STONES
(gray)

DAY 18: Daniel/Lion's Den

Opening Activity: Have everyone in the family take turns making animal noises while the other family members guess what animal it is. Have the last one you do be a lion. Say: There are some lions in our Bible story today! Let's see what happens.

Reading: "On the seventh day the king came to mourn for Daniel. As he came to the den and looked in, there was Daniel, sitting there. The king cried aloud, "You are great, O Lord, the God of Daniel, and there is no other besides you!"" (Daniel 6 or the story of Daniel in the Lion's Den)

Symbol: Lion in the den, with his mouth closed by the angel who protected Daniel

Summary: Daniel lived in the kingdom of the Medes and Persians, who did not worship God. A rule in the kingdom was made that its people could only pray to the king; Daniel continued praying to God as he had always done. Several of the supervisors and satraps that worked for the king felt outshone by Daniel, as Daniel was filled with the Holy Spirit. They turned Daniel in for praying to God, and Daniel was sentenced to the lion's den. God protected Daniel, keeping him safe. When the king came to the den the next day, he found that God had protected Daniel and kept him safe. He realized the greatness of God, and declared God's power to all the nations.

Jesus Connection: Daniel was accused of doing something wrong even though he was only praying to God. He was thrown into the lion's den as a punishment. But Daniel trusted God to save him from death, and God closed the mouth of the lions. We aren't in danger of lions, but we do face the punishment of death for our sins. We can trust God to save us from the punishment of death—being forever separated from God after we die— because Jesus took the punishment for our sins. We believe in Jesus as our Savior and need to follow His lead as our Lord.

Prayer: Let's thank God for being trustworthy. We can thank Him for saving Daniel in the lion's den and for saving us from the punishment of death. (Example: Thank You, God, that I can trust You. Thank you for saving Daniel from the lions and providing a way to save me. Please help me live my life for You. I want You to be glorified through everything I think, say and do. I love You. Amen.)

DAY 18: Daniel/Lion's Den

Materials:
- embroidery needles
- stuffing
- scissors
- felt in gray, black, tan, brown, white, and flesh
- embroidery floss in black, brown, tan, white, and gold

How to Make:
- BACKGROUND: cut out two background caves from the black felt (one for the back and one for the front of the ornament).
- FRONT OF CAVE: cut out the front of the cave from the gray felt, leaving the doorway open/cut out.
- ANGEL: cut out the angel (circle from flesh tone felt for head, triangle with rounded edges from white felt for body). Attach the body to the gray cave using a straight stitch. To attach the head, place a drop of glue at the back (optional) and secure it down with gold thread to form the halo.
- LION: cut out a face, mane, and body for your lion from the tan and brown felt. Lay the gray cave down on top of the black background, and position the lion in the doorway. Stitch the lion down into the doorway onto the top of the black felt in this order: body (brown), mane (tan), head (brown).
- ATTACHING FRONT TO BACK: lay the felt piece you've been working with on top of the remaining black background, and blanket stitch the three pieces together. Be sure to add some stuffing just before you sew it closed!

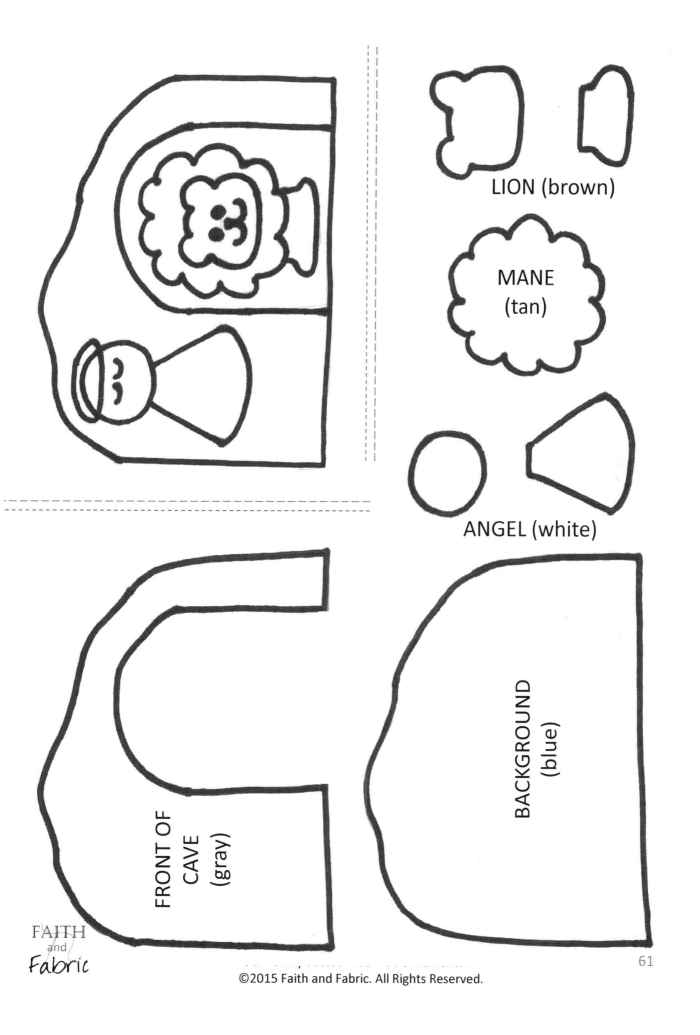

LION (brown)

MANE
(tan)

ANGEL (white)

FRONT OF CAVE (gray)

BACKGROUND (blue)

FAITH
and
Fabric

61

DAY 19: Jonah in the whale

Opening Activity: Draw a large fish on a piece of paper and tape the paper to your wall. Draw a small stick figure on another paper and cut him out. Put a bubble of tape on the back of the stick figure and take turns sticking Jonah on the fish. If your children are older, blindfold them and spin them around before they take their turns. Say: Today, we're going to read about someone who gets swallowed by a fish!

Reading: "Now the LORD provided a huge fish to swallow Jonah, and Jonah was in the belly of the fish three days and three nights" (Jonah 1-4 or the story of Jonah)

Symbol: Whale (huge fish)

Summary: Johan was a prophet, sent by God to bring God's message to the people of Ninevah. Jonah disobeyed God, and God punished Noah by having him swallowed by a giant fish. In the belly of the fish for three days, Jonah realized the mistake he made. God forgave him, and again sent him to Ninevah to bring His message to them. This shows that God wants everyone (even those outside Israel) to know Him, leave their sinful life, and follow Him.

Jesus Connection: The story of Jonah is a big clue about Jesus. In fact, Jesus even compares Himself to Jonah! (Matthew 12:40) Just as Jonah was in the belly of the fish for three days and three nights, Jesus would die and be buried for three days and three nights. But Jonah didn't stay in the belly of the fish, and Jesus didn't stay dead! After three days, the fish spit Jonah out. And after three days, Jesus rose from the dead! After Jonah was spit out, he told a nation who wasn't Israel (God's special people) to stop sinning and start following God. After Jesus rose from the dead, the good news of Jesus spread to nations that weren't Israel. And the good news will keep spreading until people from every nation believe in Jesus!

Prayer: Let's thank God for clues about Jesus He gives us in the Old Testament, and thank Jesus that His salvation is available to all people from all nations. (Example: Dear God, thank You for giving clues about Jesus, way before He was born. And thank You, Jesus, for Your gift of salvation. Please help me tell others about Your gift and live for You. I love You. Amen.)

FAITH and Fabric

DAY 19: Jonah in the whale

Materials:
- embroidery needles
- stuffing
- scissors
- felt in blue and gray
- embroidery floss in blue and black

How to Make:
- OCEAN: cut out two large teardrop background shapes from the blue felt (one for the back and one for the front of the ornament).
- WHALE: cut out the whale from the gray felt. Using the black floss, sew two black eyes (French knots) onto the whale. Using black floss, stitch the whale onto the front of one of the blue ocean shapes.
- ATTACHING FRONT TO BACK: blanket stitch the two blue oceans together. Be sure to add some stuffing just before you sew it closed!

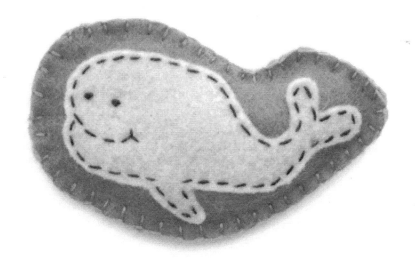

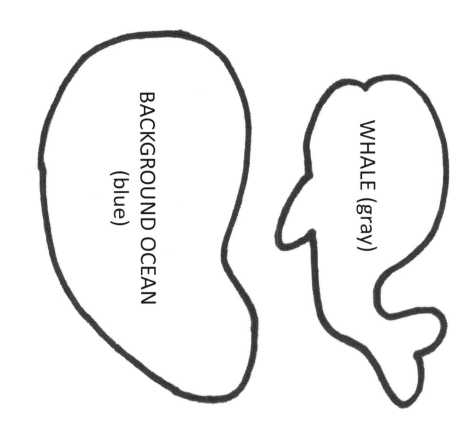

BACKGROUND OCEAN
(blue)

WHALE (gray)

DAY 20: John the Baptist

Opening Activity: Play charades with your family, making sure nobody says any words or noises while acting. You may need to whisper ideas in your child's ear on what to act out. Say: In our Bible story today, God makes it so a man can't speak!

Reading: "I baptize you with water for repentance. But after me comes one who is more powerful than I, whose sandals I am not worthy to carry. He will baptize you with the Holy Spirit and fire." (Matthew 3:11) For the story of John the Baptist's birth, read Luke 1:1-25, 57-80.

Symbol: baptismal shell with three drops of water (the Father, the Son, and the Holy Spirit)

Summary: John fulfilled Old Testament prophecies as the voice in the wilderness; God's people were waiting for a prophet to bring news, and John brought that news to them. God still reigned in His people's hearts, and John urged them to acknowledge their sins as they were baptized in the Jordan river. He told them of one, greater than he, who was to come and would baptize them with the Holy Spirit.

Jesus Connection: God had a special plan for John before he was even born. In fact, God even gives His people a clue about John hundreds of years before John is born. One of the clues says, "I am going to send my Messenger, and he will clear the way before Me. And the Lord, whom you seek, will suddenly come to His temple..." (Malachi 3:1) John would grow up and prepare the way for Jesus! He would teach the people that the kingdom of God was near. He would tell the people that they need to repent—turn away from their sins. And when Jesus starts His ministry, John the Baptist would proclaim that Jesus is the Lamb of God who takes away the sins of the world. John would also be the one to baptize Jesus.

DAY 20: John the Baptist

Prayer: Let's thank God that He had a special plan from the very beginning of the world to rescue us from the punishment of our sins and make our relationship right again with Him. (Example: Thank You, God, for having a special plan to rescue me. I'm glad I now can know You. I love You. Amen.) ***Alternate****:* Let's thank God for washing away our sins at the time of our own baptism. (Example: Thank You, God, for bringing me into your family through Baptism and washing away my Original sin. I love you. Amen.)

Materials:
* embroidery needles
* stuffing
* scissors
* felt in dark blue, light blue, and cream
* embroidery floss in dark blue, light blue, and tan

How to Make:
* BACKGROUND: cut out two background circles from the dark blue felt (one for the back and one for the front of the ornament).
* SHELL: cut out the shell from the cream felt. Sew it onto one of the dark blue felt circles.
* WATER: cut out three drops of water from the lighter blue felt, and sew them onto the dark blue background beside the shell. For the river water, cut the water from the lighter blue felt, trimming it to fit exactly around the bottom of your circle, resting just below the shell. See photo for details.
* ATTACHING FRONT TO BACK: blanket stitch the two dark blue background circles together. Be sure to add some stuffing just before you sew it closed!

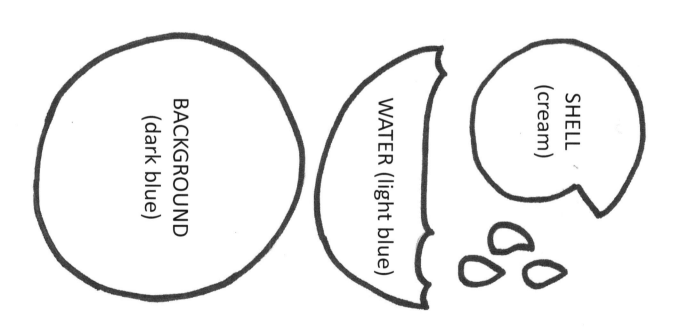

BACKGROUND (dark blue)

WATER (light blue)

SHELL (cream)

DAY 21: Mary, Jesus's Mother

Opening Activity: Prior to devotion time, get a special treat that your whole family will enjoy. Wrap it in paper. Then wrap it in paper again. Repeat many times. Sit in a circle and play music or set a timer. Whenever you stop the music or the timer goes off, the person holding the present gets to unwrap one of the layers. Continue until the present is open, and you all enjoy the treat. Say: In today's Bible story, a woman gets an incredible surprise.

Reading: "You will conceive and give birth to a son, and you are to call him Jesus. He will be great and will be called the Son of the Most High. The Lord God will give him the throne of his father David, and he will reign over Jacob's descendants forever; his kingdom will never end." (Luke 1:26-56 or the story of Mary)

Symbol: Mary holding baby Jesus

Summary: Mary is the perfect example of obedience to and trust in the Lord. A young, unwed virgin, she was betrothed to Joseph (of the house of David). An angel appeared to her, announcing that she was pregnant with the Son of the Most High - but should not be troubled for she was favored and the Lord was with her. Mary bows to God's command, and said, "Behold, I am the handmaid of the Lord. May it be done to me according to Your will." Her soul magnified not herself, but the Lord.

Jesus Connection: God had a special plan for Mary. He even gave a clue about her hundreds of years before she was born. Isaiah 7:14 says, "Therefore the Lord Himself will give you a sign: The virgin will conceive and give birth to a son, and will call Him Immanuel." Even though Mary had never been married and had never had a baby before, God was giving her a baby in her belly. It was a miracle! The baby would be God's Son, the Savior of the world! Because Jesus is God the Son and because He comes down to earth as a baby in a mom's belly, Jesus is both God and human. Because He is a human, He could live a perfect life and take the punishment for our sins. Because He is God, He was born without a sin nature, could defeat death, rise again, and give us His perfection.

DAY 21: Mary, Jesus's Mother

Prayer: Let's thank Jesus that He is fully God and fully man. (Example: Thank You, Jesus, for being both God and man. It is pretty amazing that you were once my age. Help me to obey God like You did. I love You. Amen.)

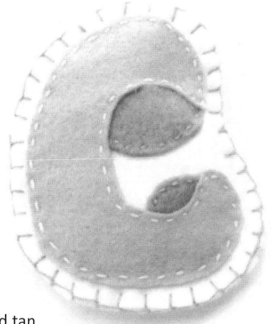

Materials:
- embroidery needles
- stuffing
- scissors
- felt in white, light blue, and tan
- embroidery floss in white, light blue, and tan
- background music: Mary, Did You Know?

How to Make:
- BACKGROUND: cut out two background shapes from the white felt (one for the back and one for the front of the ornament).
- FACES: cut out the two faces (one for Mary, one for Jesus) and set aside.
- BODY: cut out the abstract body shape from the light blue felt. Place it on the background shape and arrange the faces beneath the body shape so the faces are slightly covered by the body shape. Remove the body and stitch the faces down with tan floss. Place the body back down and stitch in place with the blue floss.
- ATTACHING FRONT TO BACK: blanket stitch the two white background shapes together. Be sure to add some stuffing just before you sew it closed!

FAITH
and
Fabric

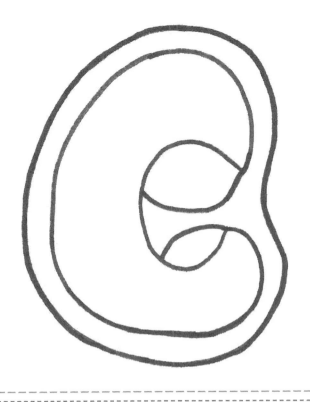

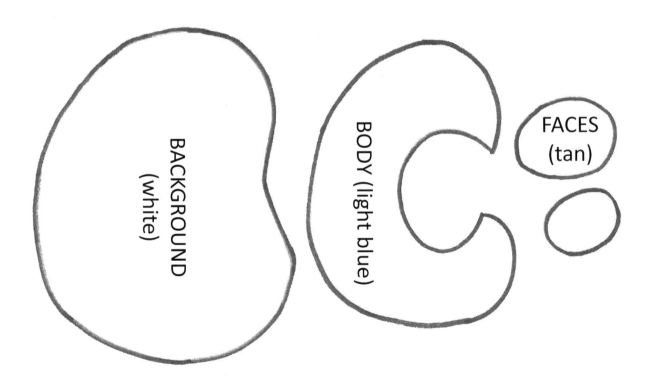

BACKGROUND
(white)

BODY (light blue)

FACES
(tan)

DAY 22: Joseph, Jesus's Father

Opening Activity: Show your children pictures from your wedding (and/or their grandparent's wedding). Say: In our Bible story today, Joseph needs to choose whether or not he will still get married to Mary.

Reading: "...an angel of the Lord appeared to him in a dream and said, "Joseph son of David, do not be afraid to take Mary home as your wife, because what is conceived in her is from the Holy Spirit. She will give birth to a son, and you are to give him the name Jesus, because he will save his people from their sins." All this took place to fulfill what the Lord had said through the prophet: "The virgin will conceive and give birth to a son, and they will call him Immanuel" (which means "God with us"). When Joseph woke up, he did what the angel of the Lord had commanded him and took Mary home as his wife. (Matthew 1:19-25)

Symbol: Wedding rings symbolizing the union of Mary and Joseph

Summary: Joseph was a kind, caring man. It is understandable that he was very troubled in finding out that his betrothed, Mary, was pregnant when he knew he had no relations with her! God sent an angel to speak with Joseph in a dream and assure him that it was His will that Mary bear His child – and that Joseph should still take her as his wife. Joseph did as God commanded.

Jesus Connection: Joseph was upset when he heard Mary was going to have a baby. But then he learned that the baby was God's Son, and God had an important job for him to do. Even though Joseph wasn't Jesus' father by birth, he was still chosen to be Jesus' dad here on earth. When building the family tree of Jesus, the Bible follows Joseph's family (Matthew 1). Because Joseph was the great, great, great far off grandson of Jesse and David, all of the clues God gave about Jesus being from their family came true.

Prayer: Let's thank God for sending Jesus! (Example: Dear God, it is pretty amazing that you had such a big plan of salvation from the very beginning. Please help me to, like Joseph, follow the path you have planned for me. I love you, Amen!)

FAITH
and
Fabric

DAY 22: Joseph, Jesus's Father

Materials:
- embroidery needles
- stuffing
- scissors
- felt in red, yellow, and white
- embroidery floss in white and gold

How to Make:
- BACKGROUND: cut out two hearts from the red felt (one for the back and one for the front of the ornament).
- RINGS: cut out the two rings from the yellow felt. Sew both onto the heart, overlapping a bit at the center with gold floss. Sew the diamond on the smaller ring with the white floss.
- ATTACHING FRONT TO BACK: blanket stitch the two red hearts together. Be sure to add some stuffing just before you sew it closed!

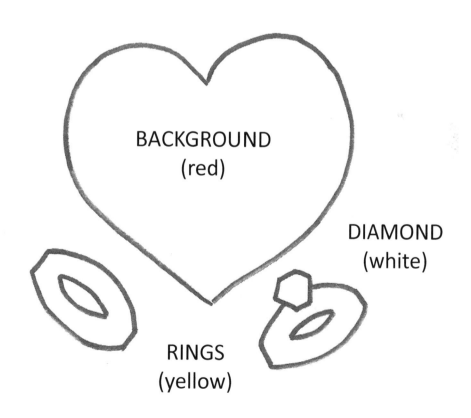

BACKGROUND
(red)

DIAMOND
(white)

RINGS
(yellow)

DAY 23: Three Magi/Star

Opening Activity: Cut a star out of paper. If you have glitter, make it shine! Play follow the leader, having the leader hold the star up while the rest of the family follows wherever the star goes. Say: Today we are learning about men who followed a special star.

Reading: "After Jesus was born in Bethlehem in Judea, during the time of King Herod, Magi from the east came to Jerusalem and asked, "Where is the one who has been born king of the Jews? We saw his star when it rose and have come to worship him." (Matthew 2 or the story of the Magi/Wise Men)

Symbol: Star of Bethlehem, which the magi followed to find the Christ child

Summary: For many years, the magi had studied the stars, waiting for a special sign to appear and signify that the new king had come. When they saw the star, they were overjoyed! They traveled for many months, following the star, so that they could meet the new king – Jesus Christ. Upon meeting him, they fell down in worship and offered him gifts of gold, frankincense, and myrrh – making them the first to worship Him and offer Him sacrifice.

Jesus Connection: In the early pages of our Bible, God hints about a star that will one day come (Numbers 25:17). The wise men knew that this star meant that God's promised Savior had finally been born! Since they had to travel a long way, Jesus was already living in a house when the wise men brought gifts and worshipped Him. What are gifts that we can give to Jesus?

Prayer: Let's thank God for Jesus and ask Him to help us give special gifts to Jesus, too. (Example: Dear God, please help me think of gifts that I can give to Jesus. I want to show my love for You, Jesus, in everything I think, say, and do. I love You. Amen.)

DAY 23: Three Magi/Star

Materials:
- embroidery needles
- stuffing
- scissors
- felt in dark blue and yellow
- embroidery floss in dark blue and yellow
- background music: We Three Kings

How to Make:
- BACKGROUND: cut out two background stars from the dark blue felt (one for the back and one for the front of the ornament).
- STAR: cut out the star from the yellow felt. Sew it onto one of the dark blue felt stars; sewing this with a contrasting color, like the dark blue floss, makes the shape pop.
- ATTACHING FRONT TO BACK: blanket stitch the two dark blue background stars together. Be sure to add some stuffing just before you sew it closed!

BACKGROUND
(dark blue)

STAR
(yellow)

DAY 24: Town of Bethlehem

Opening Activity: Hide a treat for your kids and make a map for them to follow in order to find the treat. Follow the clues or symbols on the map until you find it. (Or, for a shorter activity option, show them where Bethlehem is on a map.) Say: Today we are going to learn about a journey Mary and Joseph needed to take.

Reading: "But you, Bethlehem Ephrathah, though you are small among the clans of Judah, out of you will come for me one who will be ruler over Israel, whose origins are from of old, from ancient times." (Micah 5:2) For the story of Mary and Joseph's trip to Bethlehem, read Matthew 2:1-7.

Symbol: Town of Bethlehem

Background: It was prophesized that the great ruler of Israel would come from the city of David: Bethlehem. Joseph, from the line of David, brought Mary back to his home to bear Jesus, fulfilling Old Testament prophecy.

Jesus Connection: Mary and Joseph needed to travel to the town of Bethlehem because the ruler at the time wanted to count all the people in his land. It was a long, hard journey, but God had this exact moment planned! Hundreds of years earlier, God gave a clue that the Savior would be born in Bethlehem. (Micah 5:2).

Prayer: Let's thank Jesus for leaving all the comforts of heaven and coming as a baby. (Example: Dear Jesus, it is pretty amazing that you left all the glory and splendor of heaven to come down to earth as a baby. Thank You! I love You. Amen.)

DAY 24: Town of Bethlehem

Materials:
- embroidery needles
- stuffing
- scissors
- felt in dark blue, tan, and yellow
- embroidery floss in dark blue, tan, and yellow
- background music: O Little Town of Bethlehem

How to Make:
- BACKGROUND: cut out two background pieces from the dark blue felt (one for the back and one for the front of the ornament).
- TOWN: cut out the town scene from the tan felt. Be sure to cut out the windows and doors. Stitch this down onto a piece of the blue background felt.
- STAR: cut out a star from the yellow felt and stitch it onto the blue felt, just above the town.
- ATTACHING FRONT TO BACK: blanket stitch the two blue background pieces together. Be sure to add some stuffing just before you sew it closed!

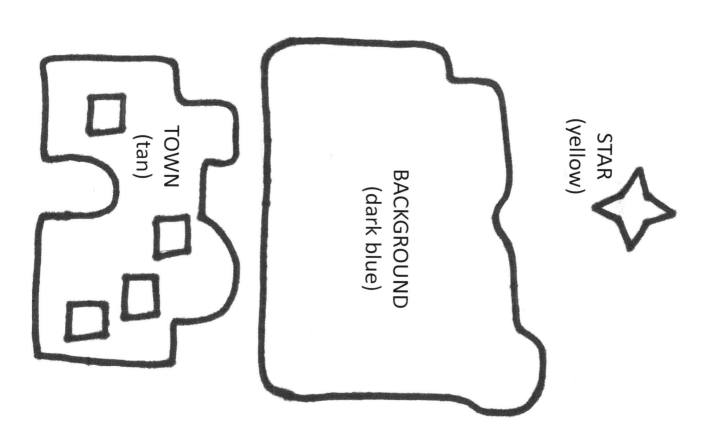

TOWN
(tan)

BACKGROUND
(dark blue)

STAR
(yellow)

DAY 25: Birth of Christ!

Opening Activity: Sing some Christmas songs about Jesus, such as "Silent Night," "Joy to the World," or "Away in a Manger."

Reading: "While they were there, the time came for the baby to be born, and she gave birth to her firstborn, a son. She wrapped him in cloths and placed him in a manger, because there was no guest room available for them." (Luke 2:1-7 or the story of Christ's birth.

Symbol: Baby Jesus lying in a manger, wrapped in swaddling cloth.

Summary: Jesus Christ was born! God has come to us in the flesh of a child.

Jesus Connection: After hundreds of years of clues, the day FINALLY came! Just as God promised, He sent His Son to be the Savior of the world. And, guess what? Every single clue God gave about Jesus came true. Jesus was born! And we know that the story didn't end there. Jesus made the way of salvation by dying on the cross for our sins and rising again so we could have eternal life. Guess what? God's story of salvation doesn't end there, either! His story on earth is continuing until one day, people from every nation have heard the good news of Jesus.

Prayer: Let's thank God for Jesus! (Example: Thank You, God for sending Jesus as a baby. Thank You, too, for having Him die on the cross for my sins. Please help me continue the good story of salvation by living for You in everything I think, say, and do. Jesus is the best Christmas gift ever! I love You. Amen.)

DAY 25: Birth of Christ!

Materials:
- embroidery needles
- stuffing
- scissors
- felt in blue, white, yellow, tan, flesh-tone, dark brown, and yellow
- embroidery floss in blue, yellow, tan, light brown, dark brown, and yellow

How to Make:
- BACKGROUND: cut out two background pieces from the white felt (one for the back and one for the front of the ornament).
- CRADLE: cut out the cradle from the dark brown felt and stitch down onto the white felt.
- BABY: cut out the body for baby Jesus from the blue felt, and His head from the flesh-toned felt. Cut a circle out of the yellow felt (the larger of the two circles). Sew in this order: large yellow halo/circle, blue body, tan head. They should be just touching / flush with the top of the cradle.
- HAY: cut out the very jagged edged "hay" shape from the tan felt. Sew over the seam created by the baby and cradle with a straight stitches.
- ATTACHING FRONT TO BACK: blanket stitch the two white background pieces together. Be sure to add some stuffing just before you sew it closed!

BACKGROUND
(white)

CRADLE
(brown)

HAY (tan)

BODY (blue)

HEAD
(flesh)

HALO
(yellow)

MAKING the Tree

Materials:

- ribbon in dark green
- felt in green and brown – you'll want 1/2 yard of brown and 1 yard of green
- sewing thread in green
- sewing machine (this is a nice, easy, inexpensive model and one I love!)
- construction cone – I used a 36" cone
- green buttons
- glue
- stuffing
- scissors

How to Make:

- STEP 1 - BASE: cut the brown felt about five inches wider than the base of the cone as shown in the photo so you end up with a large brown square. Then, in the very center of the brown square, cut a hole (approximately 5", but it depends on how wide your cone is) so the brown felt slides down to ALMOST the bottom of the cone. You want to have at least 6" of brown on the actual cone so it looks like the stem of the tree. **TIP**: start with a small hole, and then slowly make it larger as you can't "go back" if you cut it to big. Once you have the desired shape and like the way the brown felt sits on the cone, gather the extra felt under the base. Glue it down in an organic style (let it bunch) to both the stem of the cone, base, and underneath the base. Use a few stitches for extra stability in holding it in place.
- STEP 2 - BRANCHES: as shown in the photo, cut a curve/wave pattern out of the green felt. You'll want the length of the curved piece to be about four inches WIDER than the circumference of the cone so it can overlap and be stitched together to form a ring. Cut out two matching wave pieces, and stitch them together along the bottom of the curve (leave the top open). Put a bit of stuffing in each curve to puff it out a bit. You will repeat this multiple times, as each "ring of waves" is a separate layer – the rings will also get smaller and smaller as you get closer to the top. Make the rings one layer at a time, pinning them around the tree, and – once you like the arrangement - going back and hand-stitching them into place.
- STEP 3 - BUTTONS: attach buttons (25 in total) randomly on the tree so you have a place to hang the ornaments.

FAITH
and
Fabric

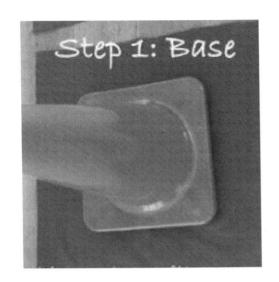

Step 1: Base

Step 2: Branch

Jesse Tree

FAITHandFabricdesign.com

FAITH and Fabric

For more faith-inspired family fun throughout the year, check out:

Family Activities for Lent and Easter:
Over 40 pages of Projects, Opening
Discussions, and Closing Talks to
celebrate Ash Wednesday, Holy Week,
Triduum, and Easter Sunday!

http://etsy.me/1KSCCJS

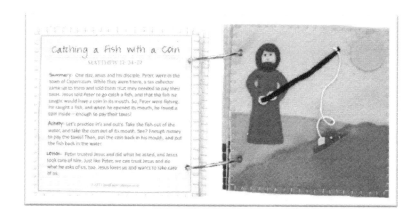

Felt Bible Activities Book:
Create your own interactive felt activity
book for your little one! They'll have fun
learning about Jesus's miracles, while
practicing small hand skills like buttons,
snaps, velcro, pinching, and pulling.

http://etsy.me/2akNgTk

Made in the USA
Columbia, SC
06 November 2018